"ALL BELIEVERS IN CHRIST NEED THE REMINDER TO REMEMBER THE BASICS OF OUR FAITH AND THE TRUTHS OF CHRIST. NEW BELIEVERS IN PARTICULAR NEED A CLEAR AND CONCISE EXPLANATION OF THE BASICS OF THE GOSPEL BOTH IN ORIGIN AND RESULTS. THIS BOOK IS A VERY A COMPLETE COMPILATION OF TRUTHS TO KEEP BELIEVERS ON COURSE AND IN FULL FAITH. NOT ONLY WOULD I RECOMMEND THIS FOR YOUNG BELIEVERS, I WOULD ALSO RECOMMEND THAT ALL BELIEVERS REREAD IT FROM TIME TO TIME TO BE ASSURED OF WHAT GOD'S WORD TEACHES."

Dr. David Knapp, adjunct professor Global Grace Seminary
author of *I Didn't know What to Say*

"THE AUTHOR TAKES A VERY IMPORTANT AND OFTEN MISUNDERSTOOD SUBJECT AND PRESENTS IT IN SUCH A WAY THAT NOT ONLY WILL A NEW BELIEVER BENEFIT FROM ITS STUDY BUT ALSO ONE WHO HAS BEEN SAVED FOR A LENGTH OF TIME. MUCH OF CHRISTIANITY SUFFERS FROM A LACK OF UNDERSTANDING POSITIONAL TRUTHS AS PUT FORTH IN THIS BOOK. I WOULD HIGHLY RECOMMEND THE USE OF THIS STUDY MATERIAL."

Dr. Noel Mayes, Pastor, Maple Ridge Bible Church

AFTER RETIRING FROM THE INSTITUTE FOR CREATION RESEARCH, MY WIFE AND I ATTENDED THE BIBLE SCHOOL WHERE ERNIE RICHARDS WAS TEACHING. IN A VERY SHORT TIME, ERNIE BECAME A FAVORITE TEACHER AND DEAR FRIEND. *GROWING IN GRACE* WONDERFULLY IDENTIFIES THE PASSION OUR LORD HAS FOR US, THE DESIRE HE HAS FOR US TO WALK IN FELLOWSHIP WITH HIM, AND THE MEANS BY WHICH HE WILL ACCOMPLISH THAT WALK. WE ARE TO *KNOW* HIM THROUGH HIS WORD, *RECKON* IT TO BE TRUE, AND THEN *YIELD* TO HIM (ROM. 6)... ALLOWING HIM TO BRING ABOUT THE CHANGES IN OUR LIVES THAT WILL ENABLE HIM TO REVEAL HIS GLORY IN AND THROUGH US. THE BIBLICAL PRINCIPLES EXPLAINED IN *GROWING IN GRACE* CONTINUE TO HAVE A LIFE–CHANGING IMPACT ON ME FOR WHICH I WILL BE ETERNALLY GRATEFUL.

Thomas L. Manning, The Institute for Creation Research (retired)

Growing in Grace

Eight Biblical studies to help establish believers in Christ

Ernest Richards

Abide Above Publishing

Growing In Grace:
Biblical Studies to Help Establish Believers in Christ

Copyright © 2017 by Ernest Richards

First Printing: 2017

ISBN 978-0-9984120-1-6

Abide Above Publishing
915 N Hartwell Ave
Waukesha, WI 53186

World Wide Web: www.ehrichards.com

Email: info@ehrichards.com

All Scripture quotations, unless otherwise indicated, are taken from the Holy Bible, King James Version which is in the public domain and may be quoted freely.

Design: Christine McBride

Printed in the United States of America

Ordering Information:
Special discounts are available on quantity purchases by corporations, associations, educators, and others. For details, contact the publisher at the above listed address.

U.S. trade bookstores and wholesalers:
Please contact Abide Above Publishing at Tel: (224) 304-GROW
Tel (224) 304-4769 or email info@ehrichards.com.

Dedicated to my niece, Jennifer Bennett,
whose eager questions finally changed this project
from a "must get around to someday" to a "must do right now!"

MILES J. STANFORD
CHRISTIAN CORRESPONDENCE

840 Vindicator Dr., #111
Colorado Springs, CO 80919

5 September 1998

Br'er Ernie

Thank you for sharing your new <u>Growing in Grace</u>.

It is well done--concise and comprehensive. Only those who know
their subject can do that.

It should be very effective both for the new believer, and the
helper.

Resting in Him,

Contents

Please read this first --

Let me *warmly* welcome you to the family of God!

You're reading this book now because you have made a decision. Someone shared with you the message we call "the gospel," the good news of salvation in Jesus Christ. You believed that good news and put your trust in the work that Jesus of Nazareth, God's only begotten Son, finished for you on the cross of Calvary. Through your faith in Christ's work, you've become a child of God.

Let me elaborate . . . At a certain point in time, you came to understand and embrace *three crucial issues*. One, you saw yourself as God saw you, a convicted sinner with no defense against the just condemnation of a holy God. You saw yourself as cut off from the life of God because of your sins and headed for an eternity in Hell unless something could be done to save you. Two, you saw from the Bible that there was nothing you could do to save yourself, but that Christ went to the Cross and allowed Himself to be put to death there that He might perfectly pay the penalty for your sin. You saw that He rose from the dead so that all the universe could witness His complete victory over sin and death in order that we might be made alive through the gift of His life. Three, you learned that there was a response required from you: to trust in Christ alone and the perfect work He did as the sufficient payment for your sins. You made that choice. You believed the facts, put your trust in Christ and immediately received God's free gift of eternal life.

This book is about the message by which you were saved and all that will mean to you in an eternity of tomorrows. Many, many wonderful things happened to you as a result of this one decision and you will never stop learning about those things and singing God's praises for them! Do you realize that how well you invest your days on earth in view of eternity depends on how well you learn these truths and take them to heart and live by them?

Get used to seeing the various parts of the gospel message repeated throughout these pages. It's a powerful, inexhaustible and life-changing message that can be misunderstood, counterfeited, twisted and watered-down but can never be worn out. This book is more about the amazing things God has done for you for His own Name's sake than it is about what you can or must do for God. That is the message of "grace."

You're reading this book because someone loved Jesus Christ and cared about you enough to see to it that you got properly "introduced" to truths that can make all the difference in the world to you as a newborn child of God.

The one book you truly need, of course, is the Bible. The only worthy purpose of this book is to point you to that one and help you get the most benefit from it.

As I write this book, I am praying that God will be able to use it to build up believers such as you in our "most holy faith." I hope it's clear and will richly reward you for the effort you put into it. May it help you to "*taste and see that the Lord is good*," and may you "*grow in grace and in the knowledge of our Lord and Saviour Jesus Christ. To Him be glory both now and for ever. Amen.*" (Psalm 34:8; II Peter 3:18)

Helpful Hints for the Use of this Book

1. These lessons were designed for a new believer to go through under the supervision of a "discipler." This may be the person who shared the gospel with you or a Christian friend who can help you go over these things. To be a "disciple" is to be a student of Christ.

2. I've set up the chapters to be covered one per week, but you and your discipler certainly may want to cover more or less each week depending on your desire and how much you are understanding.

3. As you read through the material in each chapter, have your Bible beside you. Be sure to take time to stop and look up each verse or passage in the Bible that is referred to as you go. It's not man's thoughts or conclusions that will change your life, but the words of God that He has given you in the Bible!

4. Try to keep a notebook of some kind and a pen or pencil beside you as well. You're going to have many questions as you begin to explore your Christian faith! Write them down so you can ask your discipler when you meet. It may be important to answer some of these questions as soon as possible. Others may have to wait until later, but you can bring them up again if they're written down. Don't be too surprised if your discipler doesn't know all the answers either! Some of the questions you ask may be on his or her heart as well, and you can learn and grow together. The Christian never stops learning about His Lord, no matter how long he has been a Christian!

5. Try to stay with this book and keep meeting regularly with your discipler until you've finished it. Things may come up that will keep you from meeting and your questions may lead you to set aside these studies for a time while you study out a particular topic or area, but it is important that you get a basic understanding of all the truths in this book and that you finish the things you start.

6. Even though you may be a very new believer, it is never too soon to start praying! God wants you to learn and grow more than you do and you can count on Him for the ability and strength to study these truths, even when all the circumstances seem to work against you! Pray, therefore, for understanding and for the stamina, the desire and the time to thoroughly work through these lessons.

7. Never be discouraged at your progress in these things. God knows how much you are able to handle at any given time. He is working from the perspective of eternity, and He never grows tired of teaching you new things or repeating the old when necessary. You can trust Him in ALL things, even in the matter of your personal growth

Chapter One:
The Bible - God's Word is the Believer's Nourishment!

"As newborn babes, desire the sincere milk of the Word,
that ye may grow thereby." -- I Peter 2:2

It isn't long after labor and delivery that new parents discover something about a newborn child -- he gets really hungry! And when that baby gets hungry, he lets you know about it in no uncertain terms! As good, caring parents, you're going to want to do something about that hunger soon to ensure that your baby is as healthy and happy as possible (as well as for the sake of your own peace of mind)!

God says that a Christian ought to have the same powerful hunger for the Word of God that a baby has for his necessary milk, because God uses His Word to feed and nourish us so that we can be strong and grow. When I use the phrase "the Word of God," I'm speaking of the Bible -- God's Word for men (see I Thessalonians 2:13; I Peter 1:23-25; Revelation 1:2). Another term that is used to describe the Bible is *"the scriptures,"* which speaks of sacred writings.

Actually, the verse of Scripture written above (I Peter 2:2) was not particularly written to brand new believers or "babes in Christ." The idea of hungering for God's Word really applies to all Christians, whatever their stage of growth might be! Just as we need food each day, *we all* need God's Word on a regular basis throughout our Christian lives! Just look at what Jesus says during His temptation by Satan in Matthew 4:4: *"Man shall not live by bread alone, but by every word that proceedeth out of the mouth of God"* (see also Deuteronomy 8:3; Job 23:12; I Timothy 4:6).

It's sad that many Christians do not take the time to read their Bibles as they should. The Bible is God's heartfelt "love-letter" to you, and you are just now beginning what should be a very intimate "relationship" with that "love-letter" that was meant to last your whole life!

Long ago, God's prophet Hosea wrote these sad words to the people of Israel, His chosen people of Old Testament times: *"I have written to him the great things of my law, but they were counted as a **strange** thing"* (Hosea 8:12).

The Bible is God's heartfelt love-letter to you

The word "law" is used here to refer to all of God's Word that had been given to Israel up to that time. The passage is saying that the children of Israel, as a whole, did not value God's Word as they should have. They did not have an intimate familiarity with His Book but looked upon it as something very "strange" and even irrelevant.

On the other hand, there have always been a few individuals who have seen God's Word for the precious, timeless treasure that it is and have been able to get tremendous benefit as a result. One of those was the man who wrote the first Psalm in the book of Psalms: *"Blessed is the man that walketh not in the counsel of the ungodly, nor standeth in the way of sinners, nor sitteth in the seat of the scornful. But his delight is in the law of the LORD; and in his law doth he meditate day and night. And he shall be like a tree planted by the rivers of water, that bringeth forth his fruit in his season; his leaf also shall not wither; and whatsoever he doeth shall prosper"* (Psalm 1:1-3).

Again, the word "law" in the above passage is an expression that was used to speak of the Scriptures as a whole. The word "blessed" describes someone who is in a very good situation. This person will "prosper," which means to succeed or thrive, to become strong and flourish. This prosperity mainly has to do with our "spiritual" well being; it is not a guarantee that we will get rich or that we will never be sick if we read our Bibles!

There are just a few important things you should know about your Bible, to help you appreciate it for what it is.

First, we take the term, "God's Word" literally, because the Bible is "*inspired*." This does not mean that the human authors felt a great surge of creative genius and flair when they wrote, but that the Scriptures were actually breathed out of the mouth of God! "*All scripture is given by inspiration of God, and is profitable for doctrine, for reproof, for correction, for instruction in righteousness: that the man of God may be perfect, thoroughly furnished unto all good works*" (II Timothy 3:16-17).

INFALLIBLE:
wholly trustworthy

It is important that you know that God is the source of the Bible so that you can be confident in the contents of this book. No part of the Bible came from the minds of men, but God gave His apostles and prophets the very words that they were to say: "*Knowing this first, that no prophecy of the scripture is of any private interpretation. For the prophecy came not in old times by the will of man: but holy men of God spake as they were moved by the Holy Ghost (Spirit).*" (II Peter 1:20-21).

The word "prophecy" here does not strictly mean *foretelling* the future, but *forthtelling* the very thoughts of God's heart to men. The word "interpretation" means "unfolding" and the word "private" refers to what any one individual comes up with on his own. The idea is: no person ever invented these things and wrote them down out of his own creative imagination, but God's Spirit "carried men along," or moved them to write the very words He chose to convey His thoughts.

Because the words of the Bible came from God, they are "inerrant," or without error. "*The words of the LORD are pure words: as silver tried in a furnace of earth, purified seven times.*" (Psalm 12:6). "*Every word of God is pure: He is a shield unto them that put their trust in Him. Add thou not unto His words, lest He reprove thee, and thou be found a liar*" (Proverbs 30:5-6). God can't lie or make mistakes! The Bible is a faithful record that you can trust perfectly.

Because the Bible comes from God and because its words are true, true believers have always regarded the Bible as their one *authority for faith and practice*. This means that for the truth that saves our souls and for the truths on which we build our day-to-day lives, we always turn to our Bibles. This is the Word God has given us to spare us from the tragic ruin that many suffer and to lead us on to full growth and victory in our Christian lives.

There is no other infallible authority we are to turn to besides the Bible. Everything else is to be held up against this one reliable standard of truth (Isaiah 8:20; Jeremiah 23:28-29; Acts 17:11).

The greatest thing about God's Word is that it is about God's Son! Jesus said, "*Search the scriptures . . . they are they which testify of me*" (John 5:39). Through the Scriptures we come to know Christ, and there we discover present and eternal riches God has for us through actual *participation* in Christ's life (I Corinthians 2:9-13; Ephesians 1:15-23; II Peter 1:3-4).

Begin to search out and read all of God's great "love-letter" to you. You won't understand everything that you read at first, but you can certainly be excited about all that you do understand as you enter into this wonderful relationship with God through His Book. Rely on Him and *expect* Him to speak to you through the words of this Bible. Don't expect to be a full-grown, mature man or woman of God overnight. Now is the time to cry out for God's sustaining and nourishing food and to learn to feast, feast, feast!

Study and Review --

1. In what way is the Bible compared to food in I Peter 2:2 and Matthew 4:4?

_____

_____

_____

_____

_____

_____

2. What do you think is meant by having a "relationship" with the Bible? (You may want to read Hosea 8:12 and Psalm 1:1-3 again in this light.)

_____

_____

_____

_____

_____

3. What do the following words mean as used in this chapter -- "blessed," "inspired," "prophecy," or "private interpretation?"

_____

_____

_____

_____

_____

_____

_____

4. Are you confident in the Bible as your reliable authority for faith and practice? Why or why not?

_____

_____

_____

_____

_____

5. Look up the following Scriptures and write a brief sentence as to what each seems to mean -- Psalm 19:7-11; Psalm 119:105; Isaiah 40:8; John 10:35 (just the last part!), II Peter 1:16-21.

_____

_____

_____

_____

_____

I recommend the King James Bible as a faithful translation in the English language. It was the work of many men who were devout and scholarly and whose faith was literally tested by fire. The language may seem difficult at first, but it becomes more familiar with time, and it is worth a little extra effort for the accurate rendering of eternal truths.

If you want a study Bible with notes of explanation and other study helps, I recommend the Scofield Study Bible. C. I. Scofield was a strong, solid believer who labored long and hard in his studies. No man's words are perfect, but you will find Scofield to be very sound and helpful in understanding the Bible's message.

Chapter Two:
Faith Takes Hold of the Word of God

There is one thing the Christian must add to the Word of God -- FAITH!

This is what the Bible tells us clearly in Hebrews 3:7-4:2. God made wonderful provision for the people of Israel after He delivered them from slavery in Egypt. He gave them a rich and fruitful land and promised great blessing, but they did not respond to His promise with faith. The results were tragic. A whole generation lost their opportunity to enjoy God's "rest" in the promised land and nearly all died in shame in the wilderness. "*For unto us was the gospel preached, as well as unto them: but the word preached did not profit them, not being mixed with faith in them that heard it*" (Hebrews 4:2).

The book of Hebrews later tells us, "*For without faith, it is **impossible** to please Him*" (Hebrews 11:6). If we only had these two statements concerning faith in the whole Bible, we should be able to see how absolutely essential it is to our lives with God. The fact is there are many more such statements throughout the pages of scripture that affirm that faith is the very essence of Christianity. Therefore, we ought to learn all we can about this crucial subject.

Someone has well said, "*Faith is the arm of the heart that reaches out and takes hold of God's provision.*" God tells us what He's done for us, and what He will do, in His Word. Then, it's our responsibility to *believe* that His Word is true and trust Him to carry it out on our behalf. This is what faith is; it simply takes God at His Word and relies on Him to faithfully perform what He has promised. Faith *latches on* to the provision He has so graciously made and *clings* to it (Hebrews 6:18).

It is impossible to be *saved* without faith. We enter into salvation only by believing that Christ, God's Holy Son, suffered and died for our sins and rose again from the dead on the third day, in accordance with the Scriptures (I Corinthians 15:1-4). Scripture says Jesus Christ came and died for the sins of the *whole world* (John 3:16; II Corinthians 5:19; I John 2:2), but the only ones going to Heaven are those who receive Him as Savior by faith (John 1:11-12). Those who don't believe this message will die in their sins and spend an eternity in Hell (John 3:18, 36; II Thessalonians 1:8-9). Again, is this anything less than a great tragedy?

Faith *latches on* to the provision He has so graciously made and *clings* to it

It is also impossible to *grow* without faith. Did you know that the Christian life is to be lived the very same way it is begun? I'll say it again, because this is such an important concept: The Christian life is begun by faith, and it is to be lived the same way -- *by faith!* I stress this because many make the mistake of thinking that while God did the work necessary for our salvation, now it is up to us to struggle and strive with every ounce of *our own human strength* for the rest of our Christian lives.

On the contrary, Colossians 2:6 tells us, "*As ye have therefore received Christ the Lord, so walk ye in Him.*" We *received* Christ by faith. Now we are to *walk in Him* by the very same means.

We are to take hold of the strength and provision of God by faith, "the arm of our heart." We are to take encouragement from the truths of His Word and depend completely *on His strength* to live the kind of lives we should.

For instance, the Bible tells us all our sins are forgiven at the time we're saved, and even sins we commit afterwards will not be counted against us (Colossians 2:13; John 5:24). Knowing this and *believing it* allow me to experience real peace in my life. On the other hand, if I don't believe this, I may live in terrible guilt and fear of judgment, though my actual situation is one of "peace with God."

God further tells me He's in complete control of the circumstances of my life (Matthew 10:29-30). I can be sure in the most difficult trials that He will never leave me (Hebrews 13:5), that He cares deeply for me (I Peter 5:7) and that nothing can happen to me that won't actually be used for good

(Romans 8:28)! For reasons such as these, God asks me to "*give thanks in everything*" (I Thessalonians 5:18). How could I ever do so if I did not *believe* these things He has said?

God also tells me to "*reckon*" or consider myself to have died to the power of sin in my life (Romans 6:11)! Though I still very much experience the drives and impulses of sin after I am born-again, God says He has freed me from its control. He says that He actually lives in me through the Holy Spirit, and I can trust Him to enable me to live a holy life (I Corinthians 6:19; Galatians 5:16). This calls for real faith! (Don't worry -- we'll study these great truths much more later.)

The difficulty is I am asked to believe what God says even when my own experience and my senses tell me something contrary. I really don't *feel* "dead to sin" and I may have just sinned within the last hour! Nevertheless, the Bible says, "*we walk by faith, **not** by sight*" (II Corinthians 5:7). In other words, when the evidence of my senses and my experience runs contrary to the Word of God, I should believe the Word of God.

Hebrews 11:1 says, "Faith *is the substance of things **hoped for**, the evidence of things not seen.*" It does great honor to a person's character when we believe in them even when there doesn't seem to be any visible or tangible evidence to back them up. Likewise, we do honor to God when we believe in invisible realities based on nothing more than the *bare evidence of His Word*!

Still, faith is not a "blind leap," as some would say. It is not "positive thinking" or "pretend hard enough and it will come to pass." Faith must be based on the eternally fixed facts of God's Word, or it is not faith at all but fantasy! Fantasy may be fun, but it is not Biblical Christianity.

> **it is only the *object* of our faith that makes faith such a powerful force**

Evan Hopkins wrote, "Faith needs facts to rest upon. Presumption can take fancy instead of fact. God in His Word reveals to us the facts with which faith has to deal." True faith does not deal with impressions or "wishful thinking," but with **certainty** -- the certainty that God is a God of His Word and can be trusted absolutely!

You see, it is only the *object* of our faith that makes faith such a powerful force. It would be foolish to buy a broken-down, old lawnmower with no blades and think that if I just have faith, I can mow the lawn in front of the White House. I'd better buy myself a good, working lawnmower, make sure the blades are intact and put some gas in it. Then I can rely on my lawnmower to do the job!

What God has said and the promises He's given are true whether I believe them or not. My faith doesn't make them real, *but it does make them mine.* Faith allows me to personally benefit from God's promises and enjoy them to the full. When I believe the record God has given and truly depend on Him, I am exercising faith -- *and the results will be a supernatural Christian life.*

Thus, Paul wrote to the believers of Thessalonica, "*For this cause also thank we God without ceasing, because, when ye received the word of God which ye heard of us, ye received it not as the word of men, but as it is in truth, the word of God, which **effectually worketh** also in **you that believe**"* (I Thessalonians 2:13).

Faith is my hearty "Amen!" to God's "Truth!" As William R. Newell has said, "faith is simply lending credence to One Who cannot lie!"

Study and Review --

1. Take a look at Hebrews 3:7-4:2. What was the sad result for the generation of Israelites that did not receive God's Word with faith? (See especially 3:11, 13, 17, 18-19)

_____

_____

_____

_____

_____

2. Can you explain why faith is called "the arm of the heart?" Use Bible verses in your answer if you can think of any. Be sure to pray and ask God to help you understand this.

_____

_____

_____

_____

_____

3. What exactly did you do to be "saved?" What must you do above all to live the Christian life?

_____

_____

_____

_____

_____

_____

4. Give two examples of how faith can work in the life of a Christian. You may use examples that you find in the chapter or come up with some examples of your own.

_____

_____

_____

_____

_____

_____

_____

_____

_____

5. What does it mean when we say "it is only the **object** of our faith that makes faith such a powerful force?" What is the object of our faith?

_____

_____

_____

_____

_____

_____

_____

_____

_____

_____

_____

_____

_____

_____

Chapter Three:
The New Creation!

When you believed the gospel message, much more happened to you than salvation from eternal punishment in Hell, as wonderful as that is. God's Word says you were made "*a new creature*" (*or "new creation"* -- II Corinthians 5:17). You were "*born again*," according to the Scriptures (John 3:3). You were delivered out of the darkness of this world of lost humanity, you were "*passed from death unto life*" (John 5:24) and you were "*translated . . . into the kingdom of His dear Son*" (Colossians 1:13).

Is all this just rhetoric? No -- it was absolutely necessary that you actually be "surgically removed" from a race that is totally condemned and cursed by God to be re-created in the One who is "*the beginning of the creation of God*," that is, Jesus Christ.

Think of it. You came into this world a child of Adam, the first man. As Adam's descendant, you were to inherit and carry on his family traits. Miles J. Stanford has written, "God made Adam to be the source, the prototype, the head, the representative man of the entire race. All the human family was to spring from Adam and Eve. In that way the personhood and the human characteristics of Adam would be instilled in the race through the inherited oneness of nature."

Adam was created to express the image of God in this world (Genesis 1:26). He had a physical body, which gave him consciousness of the world around him, a soul, which allowed him consciousness of self, and a spirit through which he could encounter and enjoy his God.

When Adam sinned, he died, just as God said he would (Genesis 2:17). We're not talking about a *physical death* here (that was part of the package, too but wasn't fully experienced until much later for Adam -- Genesis 5:3-5). The immediate consequence of Adam's sin was *spiritual death*. Adam reaped death in his relationship to God. His spirit did not cease to exist, but it was cut off from God's Spirit, the source of spiritual life.

Consequently, Adam became "*fleshly*" in character (Genesis 6:3). He was unable to express the image of a holy God in his fallen state. He was no longer a "*spiritual*" being, living in communion and harmony with God's Spirit, but was now to be dominated by his soulish desires and the drives and cravings of his body. As such, Adam now had in himself the potential for every degenerate form of sin (Mark 7:21-23; Romans 1:26-32; Galatians 5:19-21).

> His spirit did not cease to exist, but it was cut off from God's Spirit, the source of spiritual life.

Adam and Eve brought forth children like themselves. We all enter into life bearing Adam's fallen image and sharing his judgment (Genesis 5:3; Romans 5:12). It's so important to see that, in God's perspective, Adam acted as the spokesperson, or representative head, of the whole human race. All of humanity was *in Adam* at the time he disobeyed and fell in the Garden of Eden.

God sees the entire creation in Adam as under condemnation (Romans 5:16-18; I Corinthians 15:22). We bear the guilt and penalty of Adam's original sin as well as our own (which, for each of us, are many!). What's more, we are *constituted sinners* by our very relationship to fallen Adam (Romans 5:19). That is, it is in our *constitution* or make-up to sin; our very nature is to follow slavishly the impulses of "*me first*!"

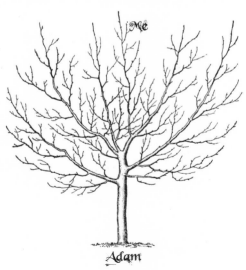

Me

Adam

Think over some of the statements of scripture on this: "*And God saw that the wickedness of man was great in the earth, and that every imagination of the thoughts of his heart was only evil continually*" *(Genesis 6:5). ". . . for the imagination of man's heart is evil from his youth . . ." (Genesis 8:21). "Behold, I was shapen in iniquity, and in sin did my mother conceive me" (Psalm 51:5). "But we are all as an unclean thing, and all our righteousnesses are as filthy rags . . . " (Isaiah 64:6). "The heart is deceitful above all things, and desperately wicked: who can know it?" (Jeremiah 17:9). "There is none righteous, no, not one" (Romans 3:10). "For the carnal mind is enmity against God: for it is not subject to the law of God, neither indeed can be (Romans 8:7).*

In spite of the sad history of this fallen race, God did not give up His original purpose of having man reflect His divine image on planet earth. However, God could no longer use the "original material" to accomplish His purpose because all that are born of Adam's stock inherit Adam's fallen and depraved nature (See Job 14:4; Jeremiah 13:23).

In His Divine wisdom, God chose to set Adam's race aside through death. He accomplished this by bringing in a new representative for the human race, and bringing that representative down into death once for all. Jesus Christ became the "last Adam" when he took our death on the Cross (II Cor. 5:17, 21; Romans 8:3). He didn't just take the penalty for our sins – The Bible says He was "made" to be sin itself for our sake!

your ties to the "old creation" had to be completely broken because the condemnation on that race is utter and complete.

You could not be acceptable to God as long as you were identified with Adam. Your ties to the "old creation" had to be completely broken because the condemnation on that race is utter and complete. Adam is not "up for consideration" any longer; there is another Man Who is completely accepted by God and is the object of His love. All who are identified with Him are accepted and loved as well (Matthew 3:17; Ephesians 1:6; Romans 8:38-39).

29

When you put your faith in Christ, God identified you with the "last Adam." He included you in His own death on the Cross (Romans 6:3). You were cut off from the life of the first Adam and re-created as a member of *the creation of God*," a partaker of the divine nature and life (II Peter 1:4). In God's eyes, we are no longer in Adam, but "*in Christ!*" Where the Father sees Christ, He sees you also!

When you trusted Christ, you did more than receive salvation -- *you received the Savior*. "God gave you eternal life by giving you His Son Who is *life eternal*." The Lord Jesus Christ has actually taken up residence in you in the person of the Holy Spirit, Who is the Spirit of Christ (John 14:16; Romans 8:9). You are now in a "living and eternal union with God the Son."

For the rest of our lives, God will be conforming us to the image of His Son that we might fulfill His purpose of reflecting the image of God on earth (Romans 8:29; II Corinthians 3:18). Our part in this process is to nourish ourselves up on the truths of this new life as we feed on His Word and to trust Him to bring this transformation about as we believe His Word concerning Christ.

It's been said that the whole of Scripture is the history of two men -- Adam and Christ. Which one do you see as your identity? Which one will you make the object of your gaze? God's eyes are set on His beloved Son, the source and first-born of the New Creation. It is there we must set our eyes as well as we "grow in grace and in the knowledge of the Lord Jesus."

This chapter contains adapted material and quotations from

"The New Birth Explained" by Miles J. Stanford.

Further study in that excellent booklet is highly recommended.

Study and Review --

NOTE: This chapter certainly may stretch your capacity to understand these truths. You and your discipleship helper should feel free to take more than one week to go over it and "take it all in." As hard as it may be to understand and believe, it is all the more important that you study it thoroughly because it is so foundational to the rest of your Christian life.

1. Study carefully the following passages, which were all cited in this chapter: Romans 5:12-21; I Corinthians 15:20-22, 39-50; II Corinthians 5:14-21. Write down any questions you may have related to the doctrine of the two representative men, Adam and Christ.

_____

_____

_____

_____

_____

_____

_____

_____

_____

_____

_____

_____

_____

_____

_____

_____

_____

_____

_____

2. Do you find it hard to accept responsibility for Adam's sin? Would you have had greater success with temptation in the Garden of Eden? What do we know about the character of God from the following verses -- Deuteronomy 32:4; Psalm 18:30; Romans 3:4, 11:33? Knowing this, could Adam's temptation in Eden be anything less than a fair test for all mankind?

_____

_____

_____

_____

_____

_____

_____

3. What are some of the characteristics that can be said of a man who is identified with Christ as contrasted with a man identified with Adam? Try to think of some and write down as many as you can. You may want to look over this chapter or read through the following passages to help you -- Romans chapter 3, I Corinthians chapter 15, Ephesians chapters 1 through 3.

_____

_____

_____

_____

_____

_____

_____

_____

_____

_____

Chapter Four:
Assurance and Security!

Young Christians sometimes lack assurance that they are truly saved. This often happens when they find they are still tempted and still sin. You may ask, "how can I be saved when I still want to do the same ungodly things?"

This uncertainty may seem reasonable and "humble," but can actually block spiritual progress. Imagine the sad state of a child who is filled with doubt as to whether she is a fully accepted and permanent member of her family. How will that insecurity affect her happiness and her relationships?

Remember, faith is "*the evidence of things not seen.*" Certainty of salvation is a matter of faith, anchored to the facts of Scripture, not to feelings or the way we behave. Looking to such shifting, unreliable things for assurance is like leaving the anchor *inside the boat*. A sailor needs to hook his anchor onto something outside his craft that is fixed and rock solid. The Word of God is that sure and steadfast rock (Psalm 12:6; I Peter 1:23-25). Your eternal salvation is truly as certain as God's Word!

CERTAINTY OF SALVATION IS A MATTER OF FAITH, ANCHORED TO THE FACTS OF SCRIPTURE

We agree that salvation never depends on what we do, but only on what Christ has done (Romans 4:4-5; Titus 3:5). Why, then, should we look for assurance of salvation in *what we do*? Sworn atheists and members of false religions live ethical lives and do charitable works. Matthew 7:21-23 tells how many who look to their "many wonderful works" as proof of salvation will find they were tragically mistaken. It is faulty ground -- the ground of our performance rather than Christ's!

The truly valid question is whether Christ's work on the Cross was enough to save me. Can there be any doubt as to the sufficiency of His shed blood? Because He is God's Son, the work He finished has infinite value (Hebrews 9:13-14), it is sufficient for the "*chief of sinners*" (I Timothy 1:15), it is sufficient for the sins of the whole world (I John 2:2), and it is more than sufficient for me.

John wrote: "*If we receive the witness of men, the witness of God is greater: for this is the witness of God which He hath testified of His Son. He that believeth on the Son of God hath the witness in himself* (ASSURANCE!): *he that believeth not God hath made Him a liar; because he believeth not the record that God gave of His Son. And this is the record, that God hath given to us eternal life, and this life is in His Son. He that hath the Son hath life; and he that hath not the Son of God hath not life. These things have I written unto you that believe on the name of the Son of God; **that ye may know** that ye have eternal life, and that ye may believe on the name of the Son of God*" (I John 5:9-13).

God wants us to know for certain that we have eternal life! According to John, it is a matter of *receiving the testimony* God has given concerning His Son; that those who believe on Him have everlasting life (John 1:12; 3:16;11:25). If we receive that testimony, we will have our assurance. If we do not, are we not, in effect, calling God a liar?

In the booklet, *Safety, Certainty and Enjoyment*, George Cutting uses the illustration of two Jewish families the night of the first Passover (Exodus 12:1-36). God was to pass through the land of Egypt and slay the firstborn of every household in judgment. Jewish families were told to sacrifice a lamb and apply its blood to their doorposts and lintel (the top of the doorway) and they would be spared. As we enter the homes of the two families, we find one terribly fearful and anxious, but the other rejoicing! Both families have followed God's instructions and applied the blood to their lintel and doorposts, so both are safe because of the blood. Yet only one family in the illustration knows the peace and joy of deliverance. Why? *Because only one is anchoring their assurance to the promise of God* (Exodus 12:23)!

> **HOW COULD I BECOME UNWORTHY ENOUGH TO LOSE WHAT I WAS NEVER WORTHY OF TO BEGIN WITH?**

The ones God has saved can never be lost; our salvation is "eternally secure." "*For God so loved the world, that He gave His only begotten Son, that whosoever believeth on Him hath everlasting life"* (John 3:16). "Everlasting life" means a life that never ends. If it could end, it would not be "everlasting." In fact, it is Christ's own life we receive, and that life is indestructible and imperishable!

Many fear that we can lose eternal life by sinning or turning our backs on God. Again, this ends up making salvation dependent on something we do rather than on what Christ has done. The Bible assures me that Christ's work saves me forever: *"For by one offering He hath perfected forever them that are sanctified" (Hebrews 10:14).* "Sanctified" here refers to those God has "set apart" as saved.

How could I become unworthy enough to lose what I was never worthy of to begin with? How can I "un-deserve" what I never deserved? The Bible says, *"For when we were yet without strength, in due time Christ died for the **ungodly**." "For if, when we were **enemies**, we were reconciled to God by the death of His Son, much more, being reconciled, we shall be saved by His life" (Romans 5:6, 10).* If God gave His beloved Son to suffer and die for me when I was His enemy, how could He fail to see me through to the end now that I am His child? *"He that spared not His own Son, but delivered Him up for us all, how shall He not with Him also freely give us all things?"* (Romans 8:32) Eternal life is a free gift, and God's gifts can never be taken back (Romans 11:29)!

Jesus said, *"My sheep hear My voice, and I know them, and they follow Me: and I give unto them eternal life; and they shall never perish, neither shall any man pluck them out of my hand"* (John 10:27-28). This verse is perhaps the strongest assurance in the Bible that the believer is eternally secure. If one of Christ's sheep could lose his salvation, the Lord's words here would be a lie! It would mean that Jesus was wrong when He said we could never be plucked from His hand!

Some object, saying, "No man can pluck me out of His hand, *but I can jump out of my own volition!"* But if you jumped out, you would perish, and Jesus promises His sheep will "never perish!" In fact, the original Greek words tell us something here that does not come through in the English translation. The word "perish" is in the "middle voice" in John 10:28. We have only "active" and "passive" voice in English. Whereas the active voice represents the subject acting (*I perish*), and the passive voice represents the subject acted upon (*I am made to perish*), "the middle voice represents the subject acting with reference to himself." In other words, the literal meaning of John 10:28 is *"and they shall never cause themselves to perish!"* We

35

sheep can do NOTHING to bring about our own eternal destruction!

The Bible promises us we are "*preserved*" or "kept" by God's power (Jude 1:1; I Peter 1:5) and that "*neither death, nor life, or angels, nor principalities, nor powers, nor things present, nor things to come, nor height, nor depth, nor any other creature (created thing) shall be able to separate us from the love of God, which is in Christ Jesus, our Lord*" (Romans 8:38-39).

When we trust Christ for salvation, we are "born again" (John 3:3). To lose our salvation, we'd have to be "un-born again." We "pass from death unto life" (John 5:24); we'd have to pass from life back unto death. We are "new creations" (II Corinthians 5:17); we'd have to be "uncreated." We are made "*members of His body, of His flesh, and of His bones* (Ephesians 5:30); we'd have to be spiritually amputated!

The story is told of an older Christian lady who was challenged as to her eternal security by a young cynic. "You Christians think you're so safe and secure in the hands of God. Aren't you just a little afraid that you could one day slip through His fingers?" "My dear young man," the woman answered patiently, "how can I slip through His fingers? I am ONE OF HIS FINGERS!"

Study and Review --

1. A. Describe how looking to our feelings, experiences or our good works is like "leaving the anchor inside the boat."

_____

_____

_____

_____

_____

    B. What is the one thing to which we can truly "fasten our anchor?"

_____

_____

_____

_____

2. A. Who gives witness, or testimony, concerning Jesus Christ, the Son of God? (I John 5:9-13)

_____

_____

_____

_____

    B. Who is it that is said to have "the witness" in himself?

_____

_____

_____

_____

C. What do we make God out to be when we do not believe Him?

_____

_____

_____

D. What is the record that God has given of His Son?

_____

_____

_____

E. Whom does John want to have certainty of eternal life?

_____

_____

_____

3. A. In John 10:28, whose hand can we not be taken from?

_____

_____

B. In John 10:29, whose hand can we not be taken from?

_____

_____

C. Has God given us the freedom to throw away our salvation? (I Corinthians 6:19-20)

_____

_____

_____

_____

_____

D. If we could lose our salvation, whose will would have to be overcome? (John 6:40)

_____

_____

_____

_____

_____

4. Study carefully the list God gives us in Romans 8:38-39. Can you think of one thing that exists anywhere in the universe or in time that could possibly separate you from Christ's love? If there is anything you can think of, write it down and check over the list again.

_____

_____

_____

_____

_____

_____

_____

_____

_____

_____

_____

_____

_____

_____

_____

_____

Chapter Five:
Accepted in the Beloved
vs. Life on the Ladder!

Search the world over, and you will see men and women everywhere desperately striving for acceptance. The fear of rejection is one of the most powerful inward drives experienced in the human soul. The attainment of fame, popularity and status among peers sets the course for millions of lives, and that course is the road to ruin.

As a Christian, you will never be on solid ground for healthy growth until you learn that you have the complete, unqualified acceptance of your Heavenly Father. It is of utmost importance that you accept the fact that His approval rests on you always because of who you are in Christ. You cannot do anything to lose that approval, and you cannot do anything to gain greater approval!

What you can do is believe God's Word that you have His full acceptance now by virtue of your union with His Son, Jesus Christ. You can thank Him for that acceptance and continually bask in the warm glow of it. And you can learn to esteem and cherish that acceptance and refuse to follow the dictates of the world and your own flesh when you begin to crave the acceptance of men over the acceptance of God (Psalm 118:6-9; Proverbs 29:25-26; Luke 6:26; 16:15; John 12:43).

You cannot do anything to lose that approval and you cannot do anything to gain greater approval

God gives us amazing truth in Ephesians 1:3-6: "*Blessed be the God and Father of our Lord Jesus Christ, Who hath blessed us with all spiritual blessings in heavenly places in Christ: According as He hath chosen us in Him before the foundation of the world, that we should be holy and without blame before Him in love: Having predestinated us unto the adoption of children by Jesus Christ to Himself, according to the good pleasure of His will, to the praise of the glory of His grace, wherein **He hath made us accepted in the Beloved**.*"

Isn't that an incredible passage? The phrase "made us accepted" here is one word in the original Greek language of the New Testament and means He (God) has made us "graceful, charming, lovely, agreeable!" It comes from the word for "grace," meaning He has "compassed us with favor" and "honored us with blessing" according to His own infinite compassion and love, without any regard to what we truly deserve.

How can a just and holy God do this for miserable sinners? The key is the little phrase, "in the Beloved." The "Beloved," of course, is Jesus Christ. God's acceptance of His Son is clearly seen in Matthew chapter 3 when Jesus comes up out of the water after being baptized by John. It is then that the voice of the Father is heard from Heaven, declaring, "This is my beloved Son, in whom I am well pleased" (see also the tender expressions of Col. 1:13; John 3:35; 5:20).

position
all the things that are wonderfully and permanently true of me because the Father has placed me "in Christ"

It is because God has "re-created" you in His Son Christ Jesus that these incredible things are true! When He beholds you now, as a twice-born child of God, He sees you in Christ, His own Beloved Son, in whom He is forever "well-pleased." Your position now is "in Christ," and Christ is risen from the dead, ascended into Heaven, and seated at the right hand of God the Father in "the Heavenlies," far above and beyond the sin and strife of this world (Ephesians 1:20 - 2:7).

This truth is seen also in II Corinthians 5:21: "*For He (the Father) hath made Him (Christ) to be sin for us, Who knew no sin; that we might be made the righteousness of God in Him.*" We are perfectly righteous, because Christ is our perfect righteousness; therefore, we are perfectly accepted because He is perfectly acceptable. "*But of Him (the Father) are ye in Christ Jesus, who of God is made unto us wisdom, and righteousness, and sanctification, and redemption.*" (I Corinthians 1:30.)

41

Understand that God could never accept you as you are "in Adam." That is the man that is under God's curse and deserves only His wrath. However, the Father has poured out infinite wrath on "the Last Adam" (I Corinthians 15:45), the Lord Jesus Christ. He "condemned sin in the flesh" in the person of Christ as He suffered on the Cross (Romans 8:3) so that you could be translated to the place of infinite grace and blessing and given your permanent **position** in "the Son of His love."

So "what's wrong?" Why do we still experience failure, frustration and despair in our Christian lives? Why don't I feel, look and act more like the victorious, vibrant and joyful believer I want to be? It is chiefly because my condition does not equal my position.

While my **position** refers to all the things that are wonderfully and permanently true of me because the Father has placed me "in Christ," my **condition** refers to the current state of my experience, how I feel, look and act. I find that these two are not the same. All the changes God has made in me and in my destiny are spiritual things, in the realm of the unseen, and are to be accepted by faith, not by sight or sense. As I walk by faith and claim the reality of my **position**, I am agreeing with God, and, through faith in His transforming power, my **condition** will gradually change.

We naturally tend to frustrate this process by continuously focusing on our condition rather than the truths of our position. When I am in the midst of a tough trial, bombarded with temptation, it is terribly easy to be caught up with how I am doing on earth rather than who I am in Christ.

condition

the current state of my experience; how I feel, look and act.

Coupled with this is the tendency to live life "on the ladder." Isn't it true that the way we usually look at godliness is that we must climb some invisible ladder of spiritual success? It is perfectly natural for us to base approval and acceptance on our performance. The more we do for God, the longer we can go without sinning, the higher our approval rating. If we try very, very hard and enjoy some success for a while, we have climbed a few rungs up on the ladder. If we fail and indulge in some sin, we have slipped down and must show greater resolve and try harder in order to regain the ground we have lost. Comparing ourselves with others only aggravates the problem.

Not only is "life on the ladder" terribly depressing, it is not God's plan! We need to come around to God's viewpoint in this. Our acceptance with Him is a permanent thing because of our position and is totally unrelated to our performance, whether good or bad. He accepts us perfectly on the basis of sheer grace, because of the perfect performance of His Son. Nothing we can do will ever change that. We can neither fall nor climb, because we are forever in the Son, whose rightful place in Heaven can never be challenged or changed.

Is God concerned with how I behave? Without a doubt! In John 15:16, we are ordained to "go and bring forth fruit." In II Corinthians 7:1, we are to "cleanse ourselves from all filthiness of the flesh and spirit, perfecting holiness in the fear of God." In Colossians 1:10, He calls us to "walk worthy of the Lord unto all pleasing." Peter reminds us to "be holy in all manner of conversation," (I Peter 1:16).

Yet there is a great, great difference! I should certainly desire holiness and fruitfulness in my condition, but not in order to win God's approval or acceptance. That's mine already, and it is as I understand and believe that I am perfectly "accepted in the Beloved" that the Spirit of Jesus Christ will produce these things in me, as I walk in dependence upon Him (Philippians 1:11, 2:13, 3:9, 4:13).

I'm not on the ladder! I'm not on probation, and I don't need to "earn" my acceptance! My acceptance is not based on my condition. It's not my "DO" but His "DONE!" I am to know and believe I am perfectly accepted in Christ and to take my place with Him -- *in the Heavenlies forever!!!*

Study and Review --

1. A. What does God say about the things "highly esteemed" by men? (Luke 16:15)

_____

_____

_____

_____

_____

B. List some things people (maybe even you) sometimes do to win the approval of others:

_____

_____

_____

_____

_____

_____

_____

_____

_____

_____

C. Whose approval really matters?

_____

_____

_____

2. A. What does our acceptance with God depend on? (Eph. 1:6;   I Cor. 1:30)

_____

_____

_____

_____

_____

    B. How many times in Ephesians chapter one can you find the phrase "in Christ" in one form or another?

_____

_____

_____

_____

_____

_____

_____

_____

_____

3. A. Does God always accept us regardless of how we act? (Romans 8:31- 39)

_____

_____

_____

_____

_____

_____

_____

B. Does God always accept the way we act? (I Corinthians 3:3, 5:9-15, 15:33-34)

_____

_____

_____

_____

_____

C. What two words used in this last chapter sum up the difference between the two?

_____

_____

_____

_____

_____

4. Explain the sentence, "Let the facts of your position overwhelm the feelings of your condition."

_____

_____

_____

_____

_____

_____

_____

_____

_____

_____

5. A. Based on how you have behaved this last week, where would you place yourself on "the ladder"?

_____

_____

_____

B. Where would God place you?

_____

_____

_____

C. What kinds of things do you think "ladder life" could produce in your life?

_____

_____

_____

_____

_____

D. What kinds of things ought to result from realizing our acceptance in the Beloved?

_____

_____

_____

_____

_____

_____

_____

_____

Chapter Six:
Legislated by Law
or Governed by Grace?

The Bible tells us that after God graciously delivered the people of Israel from captivity in Egypt, He gave them a Law to regulate their lives and set them apart as a nation (Exodus 19). This law included the Ten Commandments, written by God's Hand on stone tablets, as well as a system of civil and ceremonial regulations.

The Law was given by God to Moses through angels on the top of Mt. Sinai while the people stood "afar off." Moses instructed the people not to approach the mountain themselves or to even let one of their animals come near. Any man or beast that did would instantly die. Thick smoke and fire enveloped the mountain, and it "quaked greatly." A loud trumpet blast increased steadily in volume. God was demonstrating His perfect holiness to sin-polluted man.

The lesson was lost on the Israelites as it is on many today. Sinful man is blind to the fact that he is utterly incapable of living up to God's standard of righteousness. Lawlessness and rebellion is built into his frame. The Law of God rubs against the grain of an irresistible lust to live for self.

Why, then, did God ever give the law? Mainly, to prove to us our desperate need for His grace! The Bible is clear on this: "*Now we know that what things soever the law saith, it saith to them that are under the law: that every mouth may be stopped, and all the world may become guilty before God. Therefore by the deeds of the law there shall no flesh be justified in His sight: for by the law is the knowledge of sin.*" (Romans 3:19-20) The Law, holy and good, shows us what we are apart from God.

Through the Ten Commandments, many of us came to know our sinfulness even as children. The Law showed us our need for a Savior Who would mercifully pardon, because the penalty of the broken Law had been paid. Now that we are God's children,

The Law showed us our need for a Savior

48

we should be able to keep the Law He gave -- *right*?

i don't strive to become righteous; i am righteous in christ from the start

Wrong! The truth is we still have a natural tendency to sin even after we are saved. Each one of us has a "*sin nature*" that still bristles at the commands of God and insists on carrying out its own selfish desires. We may be doing quite well in our Christian lives until we suddenly are brought face to face with God's Law. We try to perform the law, but struggle terribly inside and fail to obey in spite of ourselves. The harder we try, the worse it often gets.

God knows we are still very capable of terrible sin. We are the ones who need to discover our helplessness to live righteously, even after we are born again. As we so desperately needed God's grace for salvation, we find we must look for Grace again *to live a godly life.*

God never meant for us to achieve righteousness through the Law! He intended righteousness to be provided only through His Son, Jesus Christ. "*Being filled with the fruits of righteousness, **which are by Jesus Christ**, unto the glory and praise of God*" (Philippians 1:11). "*For if righteousness come by the law, then Christ is dead in vain*" (Galatians 2:21).

Of course, a man can only keep the Law while he's alive. If he dies, the Law has nothing more to say to him. Jesus kept the Law as a Jewish carpenter in 1st century Palestine, but when He died on the Cross, He died to any claim the Law might make on Him. The Bible says God considers us to have died to the Law with Christ, allowing us to live free from its every demand. (Romans 7:4, 6)

LAW CANNOT PRODUCE RIGHTEOUSNESS IN MY LIFE, BUT GRACE CAN AND DOES

Does that mean that we are not to live righteously? Not at all. The very Scriptures that tell us we are free from the Law tell us that freedom is the very thing we need to live righteous lives! "*Wherefore, my brethren, ye also are become dead to the law . . . that ye might bring forth fruit unto God.*" (Romans 7:4) "*For I through the law am dead to the law, that I might live unto God.*" (Galatians 2:19)

49

Law cannot produce righteousness in my life, but Grace can and does. Grace is God's favor freely shown to undeserving sinners. It is God acting on my behalf out of His own benevolent nature, regardless of what I deserve. It is God doing for me what I cannot do for myself.

Not only am I saved by Grace (Ephesians 2:8-9), but I stand in Grace (Romans 5:2) and I am to "grow in Grace" (II Peter 3:18). Romans 6:14 promises me that Sin shall not rule over me. The reason for this freedom is I am "not *under* law, but *under* Grace." This means Grace is now to rule in my life in the sense of leading, directing and controlling me. Grace, not law, *governs* in the life of a believer.

> A TRUE UNDERSTANDING OF GRACE WILL NOT ENCOURAGE SIN IN MY LIFE, BUT WILL PROVIDE ME WITH THE EXAMPLE, INSTRUCTION AND EVEN CHASTENING CONSISTENT WITH TRUE RIGHTEOUSNESS

How does Grace govern? First, Grace sets me free by establishing that my acceptance does not depend on my performance and cannot be lost through my failure (Ephesians 1:6, Romans 8:35-39). I don't strive to become righteous; I am righteous in Christ from the start (II Corinthians 5:21)! My relationship with God is not one of fear and condemnation, but of love, devotion and gratitude. This lifts a tremendous burden from me and gives me the right perspective in living a holy life.

Second, Grace makes perfect provision for my failure. Though I still sin after salvation, Christ Himself is my advocate in Heaven, settling any charge against me by appealing to His own shed blood as the sufficient payment for every sin (Romans 8:34, I John 2:1-2). My eternal salvation is never brought into question. My fellowship with the Father is immediately restored when I go to Him and simply confess my sin (I John 1:9 -- more on this in the next chapter).

Third, Grace makes perfect provision for my success. The New Testament tells me I am supplied with everything I need in Christ to live a life pleasing to God. II Peter 1:3-4 says God has already given to me "all things that pertain unto life and godliness!" Colossians 2:10 describes me as "complete in Him (Christ)." The word "complete" is the same word used to describe a ship that is thoroughly equipped and made ready for a journey on the seas. Romans 8:31 states the certainty that God is "for" me -- He is not my accuser, but my benefactor and enabler! He is in my corner, actually supplying me with all I need for true and sure success.

Fourth, Grace provides sufficient motive for my success. Read Luke 7:36-50 and see how God's grace moves the human heart to utter abandon and devotion. Philippians 2:13 says, *"For it is God that worketh in you, both to will and to do of His good pleasure."* This great verse tells me that God Himself puts His own desires in my heart, *then supplies the strength to carry them out!*

Finally, Titus 2:11-12 tells me that Grace *teaches* me the way of godliness. The word used literally refers to the moral instruction of a child. A true understanding of Grace will not encourage sin in my life, but will provide me with the example, instruction and even chastening consistent with true righteousness. (Hebrews 12:15-16)

It is truly an "Amazing Grace" that is now operating in my life, leading me, spurring me on and ensuring my success. The appropriate response on my part is one of belief, gratitude and devotion. God only wants me to recognize my own need and to see Him as the perfectly sufficient One Who is ever able to meet that need according to my faith! *"That as sin hath reigned unto death, even so might grace reign through righteousness unto eternal life by Jesus Christ our Lord."* (Romans 5:21)

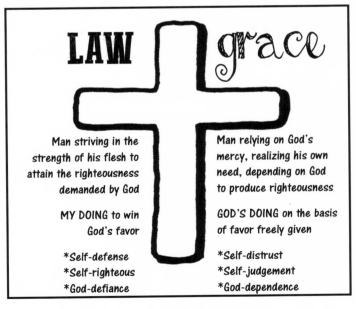

LAW | grace

Man striving in the strength of his flesh to attain the righteousness demanded by God

MY DOING to win God's favor

*Self-defense
*Self-righteous
*God-defiance

Man relying on God's mercy, realizing his own need, depending on God to produce righteousness

GOD'S DOING on the basis of favor freely given

*Self-distrust
*Self-judgement
*God-dependence

Study and Review --

1. A. What should have been impressed on the people of Israel while the Law was given on Mt. Sinai?

_____

_____

_____

_____

_____

_____

_____

_____

B. What is it about men that makes them incapable of living up to God's standard of righteousness?

_____

_____

_____

_____

_____

2. According to this chapter, what was God's main purpose in giving us the Law?

_____

_____

_____

_____

_____

_____

3. A. What do we all have that makes us insist on having things "our way?"

_____

_____

_____

_____

B. What do we need for salvation that we also need in order to live righteously?

_____

_____

_____

_____

_____

C. In Whom do we find God's provision of true righteousness?

_____

_____

_____

4. A. Why did I need to die to the Law?

_____

_____

_____

_____

_____

_____

_____

_____

_____

B. Try to write a definition for Grace in your own words from what you've learned.

_____

_____

_____

_____

_____

_____

_____

_____

5. List five ways Grace governs in the life of a believer and *briefly* explain each one.

_____

_____

_____

_____

_____

_____

_____

_____

_____

_____

_____

_____

_____

_____

Chapter Seven:
Sin, Confession and the Cross!

Yes, believers still sin *after* they are saved by God's grace. No doubt you've experienced temptation since you believed the gospel and have probably given in at times. You may have gone through a gamut of emotions following this, from perplexity to self-condemnation and discouragement.

Be comforted. This is a very *common* experience for saints, although we would not call it the normal Christian life! Although you still have a "sin nature," God has not abandoned you to its rule. He has made sufficient provision for you to recover from failure and to live in victory over sin!

The Bible speaks of salvation (or deliverance) in more than one sense. God saved you from the *penalty* of sin when He reconciled you to Himself, forgiving you all trespasses and adding to your credit the very righteousness of Christ. We call this *justification*.

God also saved you from the *power* of sin when you were born again. We refer to this as sanctification. His promise to us is, *"For sin shall not have dominion* (rule or authority) *over you, for ye are not under the law, but under grace."* (Romans 6:14) As strong as that temptation seems to be, as much "extra baggage" as you have, whatever your "temperament," or "inherited traits," or "habits," *you don't have to give in to sin anymore* – not even for a moment! Victory is yours now in Christ.

God also saved you from the *presence* of sin. The Bible's term for this is *glorification,* and it refers to the time when our bodies will be transformed in the very presence of Jesus Christ, forever delivered from all temptation and the corruption caused by sin. (Philippians 3:20-21, I John 3:2)

The salvation God has provided you with is a complete salvation, not a partial one.

You'll notice I used the past tense with all three aspects of our salvation. That is because they are *already accomplished* in the counsels of God for every believer, although we obviously have not yet *experienced* our "glorification," and are in the *process* of experiencing our "sanctification." Nevertheless, from God's point of view, all three are a "done deal"! (Romans 6:2, 8:30). The salvation God has provided you with is a complete salvation, not a partial one.

The degree to which I actually *experience and enjoy* my salvation from the power of sin depends on me. God has equipped me for victory, but I need to take up that equipment and make use of it, or it will do me no practical good. First, I need to *know* of God's provision for me by seeing and understanding what the Bible says. Then, I need to *"reckon" on, or believe* what God says, regardless of what I feel. Finally, I need to *yield*, or *present* myself to God to do His will by His power. Practical victory is not something I will have in an instant, but involves an ongoing process as I grow in faith.

Meanwhile, what happens if I do sin? I may need to be reminded that all my sins are forever taken away through the work of Christ on the Cross (Colossians 2:13; Hebrews 10:17-18; I John 2:2). Nothing I do can change my eternal standing. Because of Christ, I am forever reconciled to God (Romans 5:1-2). Though Satan may bring a charge against me, Christ Himself presents an impregnable, unfailing defense on my behalf -- *He points to His own shed blood as the complete payment for any and every sin I may commit!* (Romans 8:34, Hebrews 7:25)

Still, sin causes a problem in my *communion* with my Heavenly Father. When I sin, I am not walking in agreement with Him. I have broken *fellowship*. Again, this can never affect my eternal position, but I am now walking according to my *old Adamic nature*, out of harmony with my God.

God's provision for recovery is simple. He only asks that I *confess* my sin, and my fellowship with Him is instantly restored (I John 1:7-9)! *To confess means, "to say the same."* I am to cite my sin to God, *agreeing with Him* that it is sin, taking His side against myself. I can confess directly to

56

God; I need not go through any priest or church official. (If I have hurt someone in some way, I should certainly ask for their forgiveness as well and do whatever I can to make restitution.)

It is truly a wonderful thing that God has made it so simple to "walk with Him." It's a bit sad, though, that many never get beyond a life cycle of "sin→confess," "sin→confess," "sin→confess!" In addition to this *after-the-fact remedy*, God has furnished us with a *powerful preventative!*

God's instrument of victory over sin's power is the same as the one for sin's penalty -- the Cross of Jesus Christ! The instrument is used differently, though. In order to pay the penalty for my sins, Christ died *in my place* on the Cross, as *my substitute.* In order to break the power of sin in my life, God actually *identifies* me with Christ on the Cross as *my representative.* From God's point of view, I, the sinner, was crucified on the Cross with Christ! (study Galatians 2:20 and Romans 6:1-23)

Watchman Nee put it this way: "Our sins were dealt with by the blood, we ourselves are dealt with by the cross. The blood procures our pardon, the cross procures deliverance from what we are in Adam. The blood can wash away my sins, but it cannot wash away *my old man (i.e., the "sin nature;" all that I am in Adam)*; I need the cross to crucify me -- the sinner." Death is the only cure for the flesh.

GOD'S INSTRUMENT OF VICTORY OVER SIN'S POWER IS THE SAME AS THE ONE FOR SIN'S PENALTY – THE CROSS OF JESUS CHRIST!

My friend, these are truths that are so very basic to the Christian faith, yet they may seem very foreign to you and hard to understand. Search them out in the Scriptures, study them and meditate prayerfully upon them. They make all the difference between victory and defeat.

You see, God has *baptized* every believer *into Christ,* placing us in *union with Him* (Romans 6:3-4; Galatians 3:27). This is an invisible, *positional* truth of Scripture, not one I feel or experience. It is as if we were Siamese twins -- where He goes, I go! On account of this union, God tells me I was crucified with Christ and died with Him. This death has delivered me from the old sinner I was -- I am on the other side of the grave from him! He is held in the place of death by the Cross, while I have been raised from the dead to new life in Christ. *"**Knowing** this, that our 'old man' is crucified with Him, that the body of sin might be destroyed, that henceforth we should not serve sin."* (Romans 6:6)

> That power is the Spirit of God Himself, Who lives in me and enables me to live a supernatural life!

God no longer identifies me with Adam's race. All I received from Adam is nailed to the Cross and I am identified with Christ. As I believe these truths, I begin to experience the benefit of them -- I will know freedom from the power of indwelling sin. *"Likewise, **reckon** (consider) ye also yourselves to be dead indeed unto sin, but alive unto God through Jesus Christ, our Lord."* (Romans 6:11)

Knowing these facts and relying on them, I am in a grace position to obey God and live a life of true righteousness. Once, I habitually presented my mind and body to sin to do whatever my "flesh" desired. Now, I am free to present myself to God to carry out His will. *"Let not sin therefore reign in your mortal bodies that ye should obey it in the lusts thereof. Neither **yield** ye your members as instruments of unrighteousness unto sin: but **yield** yourselves unto God, as those that are alive from the dead, and your members as instruments of unrighteousness unto God."* (Rom. 6:12-13)

God has performed a "spiritual surgery" on me, cutting me loose from the infectious cancer of sin. Through my identification with Christ, He has put all the machinery in place to allow me to live free from sin. Furthermore, He has provided the supernatural power to operate the machinery. That power is the Spirit of God Himself, Who lives in me and enables me to live a supernatural life!

Study and Review --

1. A. We have used the term "sin nature" to describe the part of every believer that still rebels against the will of God and rises up in us to carry out our own selfish will. This particular name does not appear in the Bible, but it is basically another title for the "flesh," the "old man," the "carnal mind" or "sin that dwelleth in me." Look through Romans chapters 6, 7 and the first 13 verses of 8 and record each time you find one of these expressions used. Are there any other names given for the sin nature in this section of Scripture?

_____

_____

_____

_____

_____

_____

_____

_____

_____

_____

B. Count how many times you see expressions like "crucified," "Cross," "died" and "death" in these same chapters.

_____

_____

_____

_____

_____

2. A. According to this chapter, what three things must I do to experience the benefits of my "co-crucifixion" with Christ? Write a brief sentence explaining each one in your own words.

_____

_____

_____

_____

_____

_____

_____

_____

_____

_____

_____

_____

_____

B. What is affected by sin in the believer's life?

_____

_____

_____

_____

_____

_____

_____

_____

C. What must I do to be restored after I sin? Give a verse reference to support this.

_____

_____

_____

_____

_____

_____

_____

_____

3. A. According to Watchman Nee, what does Christ's blood do for me?

_____

_____

_____

_____

B. According to Watchman Nee, what does Christ's Cross do for me?

_____

_____

_____

_____

_____

_____

_____

C. Explain the basic difference between Christ as my *substitute* on the Cross and Christ as my *representative* on the Cross.

_____

_____

_____

_____

_____

_____

_____

_____

_____

_____

_____

_____

_____

_____

_____

_____

_____

_____

_____

_____

_____

_____

_____

_____

_____

_____

_____

Chapter Eight:
The Holy Spirit Reproduces
Christ in the Believer!

Dr. Lewis Sperry Chafer was once speaking to a class of seminary students on the heavenly, high calling of the Christian life. "Men," he said suddenly, "I realize what I'm describing to you today is a *supernatural* life. But I don't want you to be afraid of that -- *because you are supernatural men!*"

Dr. Chafer was not suggesting that his students were extraordinary Christians in any way. Actually, he was declaring that the *supernatural power* for a triumphant Christian life is present in *every* Christian. That power comes from the Holy Spirit, who lives in each and every genuine believer. In fact, any Christian who tries to live the Christian life without fully depending on Him is not living the Christian life at all.

We should know several key things about the Holy Spirit. **A)** Just as Christ is 100% God and equal with God the Father, so the Spirit is 100% God and equal with the Father. **B)** He is a not an impersonal "force;" He is a divine *person* (He can be grieved and lied to -- Acts 5:3; Ephesians 4:30). **C)** Along with the Father and Christ, the Son, He is an eternal member of the Holy Trinity, God in three persons in perfect unity. **D)** It is ever characteristic of the Holy Spirit that He shines the spotlight, not on Himself, but on the second person of the Trinity, *the Lord Jesus Christ* (John 14:26, 16:13-15).

The Bible teaches us that the Holy Spirit has a number of very important ministries, both to unbelievers and believers. We will focus on a few that have special significance to us now. First, it is the Spirit of God who *regenerates* us. Christ referred to this when He spoke of being "*born of the Spirit*" in John 3:6. This takes place at the moment we believe on the Lord Jesus Christ for salvation.

Second, the Holy Spirit *indwells* us. Through Him, God actually comes to live permanently in each and every believer, again, the moment we believe! Our bodies serve as His temple, in place of the temple of stone in Old Testament times. (John 14:16-17, Romans 8:9, I Corinthians 6:19-20)

Third, it is the Holy Spirit who *baptizes* us, or *places* us, into the body of Christ (the Church). This particular ministry of the Spirit unites us with Christ in a living way, spiritually joining us to all other believers, and planting us in our eternal position "in Christ," with all that entails! So many of the wonderful things we've described in previous chapters are true of us through this remarkable ministry of the Spirit (I Corinthians 12:13; Galatians 3:27; Romans 6:3-4). By the way, this is a "baptism" that takes place invisibly and without a drop of water. "Water baptism" is the beautiful outward picture of the spiritual identification with Christ that takes place when we are "born again."

Fourth, the Holy Spirit *seals* each believer. In Bible times, all important documents were sealed with clay or wax and stamped with the identifying mark of the owner. Such a stamp had the same legal validity as a personal signature. In salvation, the Holy Spirit is our seal. His presence is the indelible mark that we are God's children. According to the Scofield Bible, sealing represents a completed transaction (Jeremiah 32:9-10; John 19:30), ownership (Jeremiah 32:11-12; II Tim. 2:19) and security. (Esther 8:8; Eph. 4:30) We are sealed *"unto the day of redemption,"* which guarantees our salvation up to the very moment He takes us home to Heaven, no matter what might happen in this earthly life.

> **"MEN," HE SAID SUDDENLY, "I REALIZE WHAT I'M DESCRIBING TO YOU TODAY IS A *SUPERNATURAL* LIFE. BUT I DON'T WANT YOU TO BE AFRAID OF THAT — *BECAUSE YOU ARE SUPERNATURAL MEN!"***

All four ministries mentioned above are accomplished for each believer, without exception, once and for all, the moment he is saved. A fifth ministry is accomplished on an *ongoing* basis for every believer who comes to God in abject need and relies on the Spirit of God to meet that need.

The Holy Spirit *fills* believers to empower them for service (Acts 1:8; John 7:37-39), to prompt their hearts to praise, thanksgiving and joy (Ephesians 5:18-20), and to manifest the very character of Christ in their

64

lives (Romans 8:12-14; II Corinthians 3:18; Galatians 4:19). Only He can produce the nine-fold "fruit of the Spirit" in the believer's life, as described in Galatians 5:22-23: *"But the fruit of the Spirit is love, joy, peace, longsuffering, gentleness, goodness, faith* (faithfulness), *meekness, temperance* (self-control)*: against such there is no law."*

WHAT WE DESPERATELY NEED IS TO EXCHANGE "ADAM" FOR "CHRIST;" OUR OWN LIVES FOR THE LIFE AND CHARACTER OF THE LORD JESUS.

The traits listed above run radically against the grain of our selfish, depraved human nature! They are descriptive of Christ, not of Adam and his race. Man, in his own strength, may try to counterfeit such fruit, but manages to produce only a shallow, sad caricature of the reality set forth in the Bible. What we desperately need is to exchange "Adam" for "Christ", our own lives for the life and character of the Lord Jesus. To be "filled with the Spirit" is to agree with God that Adam is crucified and allow the Spirit to supernaturally *fill us with Christ* (Romans 6:6; Galatians 2:20)!

Let's be clear at once that we are not talking about a flashy or mystical experience available only to those who perform elaborate spiritual "exercises" or meet certain rigid conditions. We hesitate to use the expression "the deeper life" because what's really intended is the "normal" Christian life -- a very *practical* life that lines up with God's plan for all believers as declared in the Bible.

The truth is, He fills us as we clearly see that we, ourselves, are empty. Spirituality, like salvation, is by grace and through faith. *"As ye have therefore received Christ Jesus the Lord, so walk ye in Him"*. (Colossians 2:6) It is not something we can manufacture or develop or become worthy of. It is only as we cease looking to self and "turn our eyes upon Jesus" that *the Spirit of God* transforms us into His very image (Hebrews 12:2; II Corinthians 3:18). When we see that all we need is in Christ and allow Him to fill our vision, then, *by the power of the Spirit*, we will take on His resemblance.

The Bible tells us to *"Walk in the Spirit, and ye shall not fulfill the lust of the flesh"* (Galatians 5:16). Dr. Chafer put it clearly and simply when he said to "walk in the Spirit" is to "depend on the Spirit to do the walking in us." It is truly a matter of faith -- a moment-by-moment reliance on God, the

Holy Spirit, to do for us what we cannot do for ourselves. This is more of a challenge than it may seem since the tendency towards self-reliance ("*never say die!*") springs eternal in the human breast.

As Miles Stanford has said, "The cart must not be placed before the horse. It is not for the believer to put sin out of his life -- that is the work of the Spirit. *The yielded life is not a prerequisite for His fulness, but its result.* We came to the Lord Jesus just as we were, with all our sin; we are to come to the Spirit just as we are, with our spiritual need." Jesus said, "*they that are whole need not a physician: but they that are sick*" (Luke 5:31).

The Holy Spirit stands ever eager and able to make us "like Christ" (Romans 8:26-27)! When we refuse to let Him have His way in our lives, we *grieve* Him (Ephesians 4:30) and *quench* (resist) Him (I Thessalonians 5:19) and "Self" reigns in His place. Instead of the *fruit of the Spirit*, we will then produce the *works of the flesh* (Galatians 5:19-21).

it is not for the believer to put sin out of his life - that is the work of the spirit

As we apply these truths, it's important to see that true spirituality involves a process of steady growth in Christ. H. A. Ironside said, "Nowhere in scripture is it taught that there is a sudden leap to be taken from carnality to spirituality, or from a life of comparative unconcern as to godliness to one of intense devotion to Christ. On the contrary, increase in piety is ever presented as a growth, which should be as normal and natural as the orderly progression in human life from infancy to full stature." Feed yourself on the things of Christ in His Word *and keep being "filled with the Spirit!"*

Study and Review --

1. What do the words, *"triumphant Christian life"* mean to you? What would that kind of life be like?

_____

_____

_____

_____

_____

_____

_____

_____

_____

_____

_____

2. If we understand and believe that our bodies truly are "the temple of the Holy Spirit," in what ways ought that to affect our attitude and the way we live our lives? Study and meditate on Romans 8:9-17 and I Corinthians 6:19-20. What comfort does this knowledge bring? And what responsibility?

_____

_____

_____

_____

_____

_____

_____

_____

_____

3. Can you see specific ways in which you might tend to "grieve" or "quench" the Holy Spirit in your daily life? Study Ephesians 4:17-32. What is the solution? Study and meditate on Galatians 5:16-25.

_____

_____

_____

_____

_____

_____

_____

_____

_____

4. You may want to read this chapter over more than once, just to let it all "sink in". For further study on this great subject, I recommend "*He that is Spiritual*" by Lewis Sperry Chafer, "*The Complete Green Letters*" by Miles J. Stanford, and "*Holiness: the False and the True*" by H. A. Ironside.

_____

_____

_____

_____

_____

_____

_____

_____

_____

_____

_____